2008 How to Really Get a Date .com

2008 How to Really Get a Date .com

1500+ Websites and 500+ Specialty Websites to Meet New People on the Internet, Today!

There's someone for everyone.

Catherine E. Andriopoulos

iUniverse, Inc.

New York Lincoln Shanghai

2008 How to Really Get a Date .com
1500+ Websites and 500+ Specialty Websites
to Meet New People on the Internet, Today!

iUniverse books may be ordered through booksellers or by contacting:

iUniverse
2021 Pine Lake Road, Suite 100
Lincoln, NE 68512
www.iuniverse.com
1-800-Authors (1-800-288-4677)

Because of the dynamic nature of the Internet, any Web addresses or links contained in this book may have changed since publication and may no longer be valid.

The views expressed in this work are solely those of the author and do not necessarily reflect the views of the publisher, and the publisher hereby disclaims any responsibility for them.

All websites are currently active as of 10/10/2007.

To Update any websites or add more for 2009 Listings, please email me at Catherine_Andriopoulos@hotmail.com.

ISBN: 978-0-595-47892-7

Printed in the United States of America

To Elmo and Mr. Shark, may you be fortunate enough to get a real date.
I hope my book helps you out!

As for the bald guy on the cover, you already have a date!
What are you doing?

Contents

'My Inspiration'

The Dutch Plan Orangutan Web Dating?
(http://news.bbc.co.uk/2/hi/europe/4794279.stm)

That's all it took for me to further investigate this online phenomenon. It opened Pandora's Box to the world of dating, and the following context of my research is in an easy to use, alphabetically formatted list of websites. You too will be truly amazed with the variety of choices available today. Be single, married, or just want to have fun!

General/Popular Sites

A Single Kiss	www.ASingleKiss.com
Absolute Agency	www.AbsoluteAgency.com
Accent Dating	www.AccentDating.com
Apple Mates	www.AppleMates.com
At Last we Meet	www.AtlastWeMeet.com
Be2.net	www.Sladurana.com
Bize Bogs	www.BizeBlogs.com
Blind Dater	www.BlindDater.com
Casual Date	www.CasualDate.com
Causal Dates	www.CasualDates.com
Chemistry	www.Chemistry.com
Concerned Singles	www.ConcernedSingles.com
Crazy Dates	www.CrazyDates.com
Creative Loafing	www.Creativeloafing.com
Cupid Junction	www.CupidJunction.com
Cupid Post	www.CupidPost.com
Cupids Black Book	www.CupidsBlackBook.com
D8 Scene	www.D8Scene.com
Date 4 U Online	www.Date4UOnline.com
Date and Beyond	www.DateandBeyond.com
Date Connection	www.DateConnection.com
Date Dash	www.DateDash.com
Date Hookup	www.DateHookup.com
Date Sika	www.DateSika.com
Date.com	www.Date.com

Dateable	www.Dateable.com
Dateable Singles	www.DateableSingles.com
Dater Mate	www.DaterMate.com
Dating.Az	www.MakeDating.com
Dating 1000	www.Dating1000.com
Dating 72	www.Dating72.com
Dating Cafe Online	www.DatingCafeOnline.com
Dating Direct	www.DatingDirect.com
Dating Duet	www.DatingDuet.com
Dating Experience	www.DatingExperience.net
Dating Fly	www.DatingFly.com
Dating Key	www.DatingKey.com
Dating Match Finder	www.DatingMatchFinder.com
Dating Muse	www.DatingMuse.com
Dating n More	www.DatingnMore.com
Dating Now	www.Dating-Now.com
Dating Pop	www.DatingPop.com
Dating Revue	www.DatingRevue.com
Dating Seasons	www.DatingSeasons.com
Dating Services Online	www.DatingServices-Online.net
Dating Stage	www.DatingStage.com
Dating Stuff	www.DatingStuff.com
Datope	www.Datope.com
Designer Love	www.DesignerLove.com
Dream Dates	www.DreamDates.com
eHarmony	www.eHarmony.com
Elite Mate	www.EliteMate.com
eMeeter	www.Emeeter.com
Entirely True	www.EntirelyTrue.com
eRomance	www.eRomance.com

Eve Kiss	www.EveKiss.com
Eworld Center	www.EworldCenter.net/dating
Ez Date 123	www.Ezdate123.com
Face Book	www.FaceBook.com
Fever Dating	www.FeverDating.com
First Click Friend	www.FirstClickFriend.com
Flirt Box	www.Flirtbox.com
Foto Log	www.FotoLog.com
Found My Love	www.FoundMyLove.com
Friend Search	www.FriendSearch.com
Friends Online	www.FriendsOnline.ca
Friendster	www.Friendster.com
Fun Match	www.FunMatch.com
Galaxy Singles	www.GalaxySingles.com
Great Expectations	www.Ge-Dating.com
Get a Wife	www.GetaWife.net
Getting To Gather	www.GettingTogather.net
Googling for Love	www.GooglingForLove.com
Got the Nerve	www.GotTheNerve.com
Happy Agency	www.HappyAgency.com
Heart Detectives	www.HeartDetectives.com
Heart 2 Heart	www.Heart2Heart.com
Hi Net	www.Hi.net.com
Hip Singles	www.Hip-Singles.com
Hometown AOL	www.Hometown.Aol.com
Hookup Datelink	www.HookupDateLink.com
I am free tonight	www.IamFreeTonight.com
I Belong Here	www.iBelongHere.com
Is	www.IS-Singles.com
It takes 2	www.itTakes2.com

I want U	www.iWantu.com
Jhoos	www.Jhoos.com
Jump Dates	www.JumpDates.com
Just Great Singles	www.JustGreatSingles.com
Just Say Hi	www.JustSayHi.com
Keller & Associates	www.AGreatMatch.com
Lava Life	www.LavaLife.com
Life Long Lover	www.LifeLongLover.com
Live Date Search	www.LiveDateSearch.com
Lonely Way	www.LonelyWay.com
AOL Love	www.Love.com
Love.org	www.Love.org
Love Access	www.LoveAccess.com
Love City	www.LoveCity.com
Love Personals	www.Love-Personals.co.uk
Love Mate	www.LoveMate.com
Love Link	www.LoveLink.DiyDating.com
Love Me	www.LoveMe.com
Love happens	www.LoveHappens.com
Lovers Cash	www.LoversCash.com
Lovers 2	www.Lovers2.com
Lovers Island	www.Lovers-Island.us
Luv to Date	www.LuvtoDate.com
Make Friends Online	www.MakeFriendsOnline.com
Mars Venus Dating	www.MarsVenusDating.com
Match One	www.Match-One.com
Match.com	www.Match.com
Match Doctor	www.MatchDoctor.com
MatchMaker	www.MatchMix.com
Match Paradise	www.MatchParadise.com

Match Ranger	www.MatchRanger.com
Match 2020	www.Match2020.com
Mate 1	www.Mate1.com
Meet Your Greens	www.MeetYourGreens.com
Metro Date	www.MetroDate.com
Mingle 2	www.Mingle2.com
Mingles	www.Mingles.com
Mobile Date	www.MobileDate.com
Modern Singles	www.Modern-Singles.com
Mingled Hearts	www.MingledHearts.com
MSN Match	www.MSN.Match.com
My Happy Date	www.MyHappyDate.com
My Match wiz	www.MyMatchWiz.com
My Single Dating	www.MySingleDating.com
My Space	www.MySpace.com
Neo Friends	www.NeoFriends.com
Nerve	www.Nerve.com
Net Club	www.NetClub.com
New Loves	www.NewLoves.com
NRI Plaa	www.NRiPlaza.com
Ok Cupid	www.OkCupid.com
One Forever	www.OneForever.com
Online 4 Romance	www.Online4Romance.com
Open Friendship	www.OpenFriendship.com
Open Pal	www.OpenPal.net
Our Dating Site	www.OurDatingSite.com
Passions Network	www.PassionsNetwork.com
Perfect Match	www.PerfectMatch.com
Person 2 know	www.Person2Know.us
Personals	www.Personals.com

Personal Date finder	www.PersonalDateFinder.com
Personals Yahoo	www.Personals.Yahoo.com
Personals 1001	www.Personals1001.com
Personals Dir	www.PersonalsDir.com
Personals Finder	www.PersonalsFinder.com
Picku Up Date	www.PickUpDate.com
Platinum Romance	www.PlatinumRomance.info
Plenty of fish	www.PlentyofFish.com
QMP People	www.QMPeople.com
Rate People	www.RatePeople.com
Romantic	www.RomanticPaths.com
Romantic Planet	www.Romantic-Planet.com
Romantic Singles	www.RomanticSingles.com
Scandic Dating	www.ScandicDating.com
Sign Up for Dating	www.SignUpforDating.com
Singles	www.Singles.com
Singles Depot	www.SinglesDepot.com
Single 123	www.Single123.com
Single Gateway	www.SingleGateway.com
Singles-In	www.Singles-In.com
Single in the City	www.SingleInTheCity.ca
Singles Index	www.Singles-Index.com
Single Partners	www.SinglePartners.com
Single Personals	www.Single-Personals.com
Singles 2 Mingle	www.Singles2Mingle.com
Singles Gold	www.SinglesGold.com
Singles Lobby	www.SinglesLobby.com
Singles-Net	www.Singles-Net.com
Singles Meetup	www.SinglesMeetup.com
Single Solution	www.SingleSolution.com

Single Stop	www.SingleStop.com
Singles U Date	www.SinglesUdate.com
Singles Villages	www.SinglesVIllages.com
Social Tree	www.SocialTree.com
Solo Singles	www.SoloSingles.com
Someone New	www.SomeoneNew.com
Soul Mate Heaven	www.SoulmateHeaven.com
Speed Date Auction	www.SpeedDateAuction.com
Sultry Dates	www.SultryDates.com
Search Your Love	www.Syl.com
Take a Chance Dating	www.TakeaChanceDating.com
The Honey Lounge	www.TheHoneyLounge.com
The Love Vine	www.TheLoveVine.com
The Right One	www.TheRightOne.com
Triangle Singles	www.TriangleSingles.com
True.com	www.True.com
UDate	www.UDate.com
VIP Meet	www.VipMeet.com
Virtu Match	www.VirtuMatch.com
Virtual Dating Zone	www.VirtualDatingZone.com
Virtual Lovelink	www.VirtualLoveLink.com
Webguild	www.Webguild.com/Dating
We Make a Match	www.WeMakeaMatch.com
We Match Singles	www.WeMatchSingles.com
Wetties	www.Wetties.com
W Dating	www.WDating.com
Worldwide Romance	www.WorldWideRomance.com
Yahoo Personals	www.YahooPersonals.com
You love me	www.YouLoveMe.com
Your next date	www.YourNextDate.com

You Tube	www.YouTube.com
Yunitit	www.Yuniti.com
1st Online Dating	www.1stOnlineDating.com
101 Singles	www.101Singles.com
4 Ppl	www.4ppl.com
911 Datings	www.911Datings.com

General Dating Resources

A Book of Matches	www.ABookofMatches.com
A Good Date	www.AGoodDate.com
Abbey dating	www.AbbeyDating.com
About Lover	www.AboutLover.com
Action-Personals	www.Action-Personals.com
Adult Dating Portal	www.AdultDatingPortal.com
A-Dating	www.A-Dating.net
A 1 Singles	www.A1Singles.com
All Hearts	www.All-Hearts.com
Amore Sites	www.AmoreSites.com
Apple Love	www.AppleLove.com
Are we a Match	www.AreWeAMatch.com
Be Single	www.BeSingles.com
Biker America	www.BikerAmerica.com
Click Z Media	www.ClickZMedia.com
Crush	www.Crush.com
Cupid Media	www.CupidMedia.com
Cupids Online Dating	www.CupidsOnlineDating.com
Cyber dating	www.CyberDating.com
Datealicious	www.DateAlicious.com
Dating Bind	www.DatingBind.com
Dating Dames	www.DatingDames.com
Double Your Dating	www.DoubleyourDating.com
Dating 1000	www.Dating1000.com
Dating 9	www.Dating9.com

Dating Services 4 U	www.Dating-Services4u.com
DX24	www.Dx24.com
e2Match	www.e2Match.com/Personals
Erocity	www.Affiliates.Erocity.com
Feels Like Today	www.FeelsLikeToday.com
Find or Match	www.FindorMatch.com
Friendko	www.FriendKo.com
Fun Dating	www.Fun-Dating.com
Get Girls	www.GetGirls.com
Go Dating	www.GoDating.biz
Go to Cupid	www.GotoCupid.com
Lots of Love	www.LotsofLove.com
Love Dating Sites	www.LoveDatingSites.com
Love Links	www.Love-Links.com
Love personally	www.LovePersonally.com
Love stricken	www.LoveStricken.com
My Beloved Net	www.MyBelovedNet.com
Official Free dating	www.OfficialFreeDating.com
Online Free Personals	www.Online-Free-Personals.net
Online Dating School	www.OnlinedatingSchool.com
Online Personals	www.OnlinePersonals.com
Oversea Friend	www.OverSeaFriend.com
Personals Dir	www.PersonalsDir.com
Personals Directory	www.Personals-Directory.com
Premium Match	www.PremiumMatch.com
Prime Singles	www.PrimeSingles.com
Relationship.net	www.Relationship.net
ReStar Dating	www.ReyStar-Dating.net
Road to Love	www.RoadToLove.com
Romance Search	www.RomanticAtHeart.com

SAS Dating	www.SASDating.com
Search Loves	www.SearchLoves.com
Search Love Online	www.SearchLoveOnline.com
Sensual Date	www.Sensual-Date.com
Sesile	www.Sesile.info
Sign Up for Dating	www.SignUpforDating.com
Singles	www.Singles.com
Single Gateway	www.SingleGateway.com
Speed Dating Review	www.SpeedDatingSites.com
Tickle.com	www.Tickle.com
Toyal-Dating	www.Total-Dating.com
Try Internet Dating	www.TryInternetDating.com
Viva Dating Sites	www.VivaDatingSites.com
Web Match	www.WebMatch.com
Wally World Singles	www.WallyWorldSingles.com

Fun Sites

Age Guess	www.AgeGuess.com
Am I Dumb?	www.Am-I-Dumb.com
Are you a genius?	www.Genius-Test.com
Esoteric Forum	www.EsotericForum.com
Face the Jury	www.FaceTheJury.com
Genius-Tet	www.Genius-Tet.com
Human for Sale	www.HumanForSale.com
My Space	www.MySpace.com
Rate My Life	www.RateMyLife.com
You Tube	www.YouTube.com

Adult Sites

Adult Freeway	www.AdultFreeway.com
Adult Friend Finder	www.AdultFriendFinder.com
Adult Love Compass	www.AdultLoveCompass.com
Adult Lust Online	www.AdultLustOnline.com
Adult Match	www.AdultMatch.com
Adult Match Doctor	www.AdultMatchDoctor.com
Adult Match Online	www.AdultMatchOnline.com
Adult X Dating	www.AdultXDating.com
Amateur Match	www.AmateurMatch.com
Camazon	www.Camazon.com
Cams	www.Cams.com
Dating Online	www.Dating-Online.com
Dating Peak	www.DatingPeak.com
Fantasy Finder	www.FantasyFinder.com
Lovers Island	www.Lovers-Island.us
My Hot Mate	www.MyHotMate.com
Naughty or Nice	www.NaughtyorNIce.com
Online 4 love	www.Online4love.com
Passion	www.Passion.com
Soak World	www.SoakWorld.com
Super Fast Find	www.SuperFastFind.com
U Whisper	www.uWhisper.com
Web Naughty	www.WebNaughty.com
Wild Match	www.WildMatch.com
You're my Guy	www.YourMyGuy.com

Adult Dating Resources

Adult Dating Service	www.Adult-Dating-Service.com
Amore Finder	www.AmoreFinder.com
Amore List	www.AmoreList.com

Specialty Sites

A

Aboriginal, Activist, Actors-Actresses, Adult Swim, Adventure, Afghan, African, Age Gap, Agriculture, Aids-HIV, Air Force, Air Travel, Airport, Alabama, Alaska, Albanian, Algerian, Alternative, Alumni, American, Amish, Amputee, Anglican, Angolan, Animal, Anti Federal Marriage Amendment, Antiques, Aquarius, Arab, Argentina, Aries, Arizona, Arkansas, Armenia, Army, Artist, Arts-Crafts, Asian, Assyrian, Astrology, Atheist, Athletic, Attorney, Austrian, Australia, Aviation, Azerbaijani

Aboriginal
www.FirstNationsDating.com

Activist
www.ActForLove.org
www.ActivistPassions.com
www.SingleActivists.com

Actors-Actresses
www.ActorsActressesOnline.com

Adult swim
www.AdultSwim.Meetup.com

Adventure
www.LotsofEvents.com
www.Trianglec.com/singles_vacations

Afghan
www.AfghanSingles.com

African
www.African.Meetup.com
www.AfricanPrincess.com
www.AfricaSingles.com
www.AfricanWomenMeet.com
www.AfroSingles.net
www.BlackBook2.com general
www.EuroAfricaClub.com
www.SocialCity.co.za

Age gap
www.AgelessLove.com
www.AgeMatch.com
www.GoCougar.com
www.OlderWomenLovin.com

Agriculture
www.SinglesInAg.org
www.USFarmNetwork.com

Aids-hiv
www.HivPassions.com
www.HIVDates.net
www.PositiveDating.com

AIR FORCE
www.AirForceSingles.com

Air travel
www.AirTroductions.com

Airport
www.AkronCantonairport.com/SpeedDatingourAirlin.htm

Alabama
www.AlabamaFriendFinder.com
www.AlabamaImproper.com
www.AlabamaSinglesNetwork.com
www.AlabamaState.com
www.Alabama.Tangowire.com
www.Bamamatch.com
www.DatingInAlabama.com
www.ExecutiveAlabamaDating.com
www.MeetingInAlabama.com
www.SinglesofAlabama.com

Alaska
www.AlaskaDatingClub.com
www.AlaskaFriends.com
www.AlaskaMen-Online.com
www.Alaska.Tangowire.com
www.AnchorageSingles.com
www.DatingInAlaska.com
www.ExecutiveAlaskaDating.com
www.MeetinginAlaska.com

Albanian
www.AlbanianSingles.com

Algerian
www.AlgerianSingles.com

Alternative
www.AllWorldDate.com
www.Alt.com
www.Alternative-Dating-Sites.com
www.Alternative-Lifestyle-Ads.com
www.AlternativeMatchmaker.com
www.AlternativeSingles.com
www.PlaytimeFantasy.com

Alumni
www.Alumni.Tangowire.com

American
www.American-Dating.us
www.AmericanMatchmaker.com
www.AmericanMatcher.com
www.AmericanSingles.com
www.AmericanSpiritSingles.com
www.AreYouAlone.com
www.DateMaker.com
www.GreatBoyfriends.com
www.HotorNot.com
www.USADateSite.com
www.USAOnlinedating.com

Amish
www.AmishSingles.com

Amputee
www.AmputeeConnections.com
www.Amputee-Devotee-Dating.com

Anglican
www.AnglicanSingles.com

Angolan
www.AngolanSingles.com

Animal lovers
www.AnimalAttraction.com
www.AnimalFriendSingles.com
www.AnimalLovers.TangoWire.com
www.AnimalPeople.com

Anti federal Marriage
Amendment
www.Antiban.Meetup.com

Antiques
www.Antiques.meetup.com
www.Collectors.TangoWire.com

Aquarius
www.Aquarius.Tangowire.com

Arab
www.ArabLounge.com
www.Arabium.com

Argentina
www.ExecutiveSouthAmericanDating.com
www.FianceEconnections.com
www.LatinAmerciaCupid.com
www.MyLatinSoulmate.com
www.SinglesForArgentina.com

Aaries
www.Aries.Tangowire.com

Armenia
www.ArmeniaSingles.com

Arizona
www.Arizona-Dating.us
www.ArizonaOnlinePersonals.com
www.Arizona.Tangowire.com
www.AzCentral.com
www.DatingInArizona.com
www.ExecutiveArizonaDating.com
www.Life-Match.com
www.MeetinginArizona.com
www.ItsJustLunchPhoenix.com
www.ItsJustLunchScottsdale.com
www.ItsJustLunchTucson.com

Arkansas
www.ArkansasDating247.com
www.ArkansasSingles.com
http://Arkansas.UsCity.net
www.DatingInArkansas.com
www.ExecutiveArkansasDating.com
www.MeetingInArkansas.com
www.ItsJustLunchLittleRock.com

Army
www.ArmySingles.com
www.Fitzen.com

Artist
www.ArtSingles.com
www.SingleArtistsDating.com

Arts-Crafts
www.Crafters.TangoWire.com

Assyrian
www.AssyrianSingles.com

Asian
www.AsianAvenue.com
www.AsianCyberdating.com
www.AsianDatelink.com
www.AsianDatingFree.com
www.AsianDreamGals.com
www.AsianEuro.com
www.AsianFriendFinder.com

www.AsiaFun.com
www.AsianHearts.com
www.AsianPromise.com
www.AsianPeopleMeet.com
www.AsianSinglesConnection.com
www.Asian.Tangowire.com
www.DateAsia.com
www.FriendAsia.com
www.MeetAsians.com
www.Sunshine-International.com

Astrology
www.AstralHearts.com
www.Astropoint.com
www.CosmicSoulmates.com
www.StarMatch.com

Atheist
www.Atheists.meetup.com
www.AtheistOnlineDating.com
www.AtheistPassions.com
www.AtheistSingles.com
www.FreeThinkerMatch.com
www.MeetAnAtheist.com

Athletic
www.Athletic-Dating.com
www.AthleticMeet.com
www.AthleticSingle.com
www.AthleticSingles.com

Attorney
www.AttorneyDating.com
www.LawyersinLove.com

Australia
www.AdultMelbourne.com
www.Ausbbw.com
www.Australian-Dating-Guide.com
www.AustSingles.com
www.AustralianSingles.com
www.Australia.Tangowire.com
www.BlinkDating.com.au
www.BlueBirdsDating.com
www.Events4Singles.com
www.FastImpressions.com.au
www.FastMatch.com.au
www.FindSomeone.com.au
www.RedHotPie.com
www.Rsvp.com.au
www.SoulMades.com.au
www.SpiceOfLife.com.au

Austrian
www.AustrianSingles.com

Aviation
www.CrewDating.com

Azerbaijan
www.AzerbaijaniSingles.com

B

Baby Boomers, Badge, Bahai, Bahamas, Bald, Ballroom Dancing, Bangladeshi, Baptist, Bare Foot, Baseball, Basketball, Beach, Beautiful, Beer, Belarusan, Belgium, Bengalese, Beppe Grillo, Bestiality, Bhutanese, Bicyclist, Big, Big Boobs, Big People, Bikers, Bingo, Birds, Bi-Sexual, Black, Blogs 4 God, Blonde, Blue-Collar, Boaters, Body Builder, Bolivian, Bondage, Books, Bosnia, Bowlers, Brazil, Britain, Brunette, Buddhist, Bulgarian, Burmese, Burundian, Business Lovers

Baby boomers
www.BabyBoomerDatingSite.com
www.BabyBoomerMeetup.com
www.BabyBoomerPeopleMeet.com
www.BabyBoomerSingles.org
www.BabyBoomerSocialClub.com

Badge
www.TheBadge.org

Bahai
www.BahaiSingles.com

Bahamas
www.Bahamas.Tangowire.com

Bald
www.HairFetishPersonals.com

Ball-room dancers
www.BallroomDancers.com
www.BallRoomDance.meetup.com
www.BallRoomUsa.com/DancePartner.htm
www.SocialBallroomDancers.org/index.htm

Bangladeshi
www.BangladeshiSingles.com

Baptist
www.BaptistFriends.com
www.BaptistSingles.com
www.ExecutiveBaptistDating.com
www.FundamentalBaptistSingles. com

Barefoot
www.Barefoot.Meetup.com

Baseball
www.Baseballlovers.Tangowire.com

Basketball
www.Basketballlovers.Tangowire.com

Beach
www.BeachesBeaches.com/dating.html

Beautiful
www.Beautiful.Tangowire.com
www.DarwinDating.com
www.DreamGirlMatch.com

Beer
www.BeerLover.com
www.Zymerica.com

Belarusan
www.BelarusanSingles.com

Belgium
www.BelgiumSingles.com
www.BelgianSingles.com

Bengalese
www.BengaleseSingles.com

Beppe Grillo
www.BeppeGrillo.Meetup.com

Bestiality
www.AnimalPassion.com

Bhutanese
www.BhutaneseSingles.com

Bicyclist
www.Bicyclistsonline.com
www.CyclingSingles.com

Big Singles
www.BBPeopleMeet.com
www.BBWDateFinder.com
www.BBWPersonalPlus.com

www.BBWRomance.com
www.bbw.tangowire.com
www.BigCupid.com
www.BBWPhotoPersonals.com
www.LargeandLovely.com

Big Boobs
www.BigBoobDatelink.com

Big Singles U.K.
www.BigPeople.org.uk

Bikers
www.BikerDate.com
www.BikerDatelink.com
www.BikerMatchmaking.com
www.Biker-Mate.com
www.BikerPassions.com
www.BikerParties.com
www.BikerKiss.com
www.Bikers.Tangowire.com
www.HarleyConnect.com
www.Bikers2Date.com
www.TheBikerWeb.com

Bingo
www.Bingo.Meetup.com
www.BingoMania.com
www.iPlayBingo.com
www.SpectraBingo.com

www.ThePeopleBingo.com
www.TotheGames.com

Birds
www.Birds.Meetup.com

Bi-Sexual
www.BiCupid.com
www.BiSexualPlayground.com
www.BiWebsites.com
www.GayDardate.com

Black
www.BlackDatelink.com
www.BlackOwnedPersonals.com
www.BlackPeopleDate.com
www.BlackPeopleOne.com
www.BlackPlanet.com
www.BlackSinglesConnection.com
www.Dating-Soulmate.com

Blogs4God
www.Blogs4God.Meetup.com

Blonde
www.BlondeDateLink.com

Blue-Collar
www.BlueCollardates.com

Boaters
www.Boaters.Tangowire.com

Bodybuilder
www.BodyBuilderPassions.com
www.DateaBodyBuilder.com

Bolivian
www.BolivianSingles.com

Bondage
www.BDSMDatelink.com
www.BDSMSingles.com
www.Bondage.com
www.BondageDates.com

Books
www.BookClub.meetup.com

Bosnian
www.BosnianSingles.com
www.Dating.ba

Bowlers
www.Bowlers.Tangowire.com

Brazilian
www.BrazilCupid.com
www.BrazilianSingles.com

Britain
www.BritainSingles.com
www.UkSinglesConnection.com

Brunette
www.BrunetteDateLink.com
www.BrunetteSingles.com

Buddhist
www.BuddhistSingles.com

Bulgarian
www.MyBulgarianDate.com
www.BulgarianSingles.com
www.Velida.net
www.Sesile.com

Burmese
www.BurmeseSingles.com

Burundian
www.BurundianSingles.com

Business lovers
www.BusinessLovers.Tangowire.com

C

California, Cambodian, Cameroon, Campers, Canadian, Cancer, Capricorn, Caribbean, Car Lovers, Casual, Catholic, Cat Lovers, Caucasian, Cell Phone, Celtic, Central American,

Chad, Chat Rooms, Chef, Chinese, Christian, Chihuahua, Chilean, Christ, Classical-Music, Coffee, Collectors, College, Collegiate, Colombian, Colorado, Colostomy, Community Salvage, Connecticut, Congolese, Coptic, Cooking, Conservative-Political, Costa Rican, Country, Cowboy-Cowgirl, Cradle of Filth, Croatian, Crohn's Disease, Cross-Dressers, Cruises, Cuban, Cuddling, Cyclists, Czech

California
www.CaliforniaPersonals.com
www.CaliforniaSingles.com
www.California.Tangowire.com
www.CaliPeoplemeet.com
www.DatinginCalifornia.com
www.ExecutiveCaliforniadating.com
www.MeetinginCalifornia.com
www.ItsJustLunchCenturycity.com
www.ItsJustLunchSouthbay.com
www.ItsJustLunchTheValley.com
www.ItsJustLunchOrangeCounty.com
www.ItsJustLunchSacramento.com
www.ItsJustLunchSanDiego.com
www.ItsJustLunchSanDiegoNorthcounty.com
www.ItsJustLunchSanFrancisco.com
www.ItsJustLunchEastbay.com
www.SanDiegoSingles.com

Cambodian
www.CambodianSingles.com

Cameroon
www.CameroonSingles.com

Campers
www.Campers.Tangowire.com

Canadian
www.Alberta.Tangowire.com
www.CanadianMatches.com
www.CanadianPersonals.com
www.FastLife.ca

Cancer
www.Cancer.Tangowire.com

Capricorn
www.Capricorn.Tangowire.com

Caribbean
www.CaribbeanDatingline.com
www.CaribbeanDateclub.com
www.Caribbean-Dating.com
www.CaribbeanSingles.com
www.CaribbeanSingles.org
www.CaribbeanVibeonline.com
www.Cariblyme.com
www.ExecutiveCaribbeandating.com

Car lovers
www.Carlovers.Tangowire.com

Casual
www.CasualKiss.com
www.DatingCasual.com

Catholic
www.CatholicMatch.com
www.CatholicMingle.com
www.CatholicSingles.com
www.CatholicYoungAdults.com

Cat Lovers
www.CatLoversMonthly.com
www.CatLoversNetwork.com
www.CatLovers.TangoWire.com
www.TheCatLovers.com

Caucasian
www.CaucasianSingles.com

Cell Phone-Text Messaging/Dating
www.Clubm8.tv
www.MobileChat.com
www.MySMSChat.com
www.text-dating.net

Celtic
www.CelticSingles.com

Central America
www.CentralAmericaSingles.com

Chad
www.ChadSingles.com

Chat Rooms
www.AreYouAlone.com
www.Cams.com
www.Dockwave.com
www.CupidCams.com
www.Udate.com

Chef
www.SingleChefs.com

Chihuahua
www.Chihuahua.Meetup.com

Chilean
www.ChileanSingles.com

Chinese
www.ChineseLoveLinks.com
www.ChineseMatching.com
www.CHNLove.com
www.ChinesePeopleMeet.com
www.ExecutiveChineseDating.com
www.FreeChineseDating.com

Christ
www.ChristSingles.com

Christian
www.AChristianSite.com
www.BigChurch.com
www.ChristianCafe.com
www.ChristDate.com
www.ChristianDatingNetwork.com
www.ChristianDatesOnline.com
www.ChristianDating247.com
www.ChristianDatingInfo.com
www.ChristianDatingFree.com
www.ChristianityToday.com
www.ChristianLifeStyle.com
www.ChristianMingle.com
www.ChristianSingles.com
www.ChristianSingleSeniors.com
www.DatingDisciples.com
www.4ChristianDating.com
www.HolyPaly.com
www.IntegrityChristianSinglesNetwork.com
www.MatchWise.com
www.Relationships.com
www.Secularity.com
www.SingleC.com
www.SinglesOfFaith.com

Classical Music
www.ClassicalPartners.com

Coffee
www.BeanDate.com
www.CoffeeDateOnline.com

www.CoffeeDateOnline.co.uk
www.CoffeeMatching.com
www.CoffeeMeetup.com
www.ItsJustCoffee.com
www.LetsMeet4Coffee.com

Collectors
www.Collectors.TangoWire.com

College
www.CampusKiss.com
www.CollegeCatch.com
www.CollegeLuv.com
www.CollegePassions.com

Colombian
www.ColumbianSingles.com

Colorado
www.ColoradoOnlinePersonals.com
www.ColoradoSingles.com
www.DatingInColorado.com
www.DouglasCountySingles.com
www.ExecutiveColoradoDating.com
www.ItsJustLunchDenver.com
www.MeetinginColorado.com

Colostomy
www.MeetAnOstomate.com

Community Salvage
www.Salvage.Meetup.com

Congolesesingles.com
www.CongoleseSingles.com

Connecticut
www.ConnecticutSinglesOnline.com
www.Connecticut.Tangowire.com
www.DatinginConnecticut.com
www.ExecutiveConnecticutDating.com
www.ItsJustLunchHartford.com
www.MeetinginConnecticut.com

Cooking
www.Cooks.TangoWire.com
www.ItalianCookeryCourse.com/Singles-Vacations.html

Conservative/Political Singles
www.ConservativeMatchMaker.com

Coptic
www.CopticSingles.com

Cost a Rican
www.CostARicanSingles.com

Country
www.CountryMatch.com
www.CountryPassions.com

www.Country.Tangowire.com
www.MyCountryMatch.com

Cowboy-Cowgirl
www.Cowboy.com
www.HorseandCountrySingles.com
www.SinglesCorral.com
www.WesternMatch.com

Cradle of Filth
www.CradleofFilth.Meetup.com

Crafters
www.Crafters.Tangowire.com

Croatian
www.CroatianSingles.com

Crohn's Disease
www.CrohnsZone.org

Cross Dressers
www.DateaCrossDresser.com
www.Lvtg.com
www.Transpassions.com

Cruises
www.CruisingforLove.com
www.MustCruise.com
www.SingleCruise.com
www.SingleCruising.com

Cuban
www.CubanSingles.com
www.Cubafestla.com

Cuddling
www.Cuddling.Meetup.com

Czech
www.CzechSingles.com

Cyclists
www.Cyclists.Tangowire.com

D

Danish, Dancing, Danske, Dating with no Kids attached, Deaf, Delaware, Democrats, Deutsche, Diapers, Dinner Club, Disabled, Divorced, Dogs, Dominican, Drag Queens, Drinking, Druze, Dungeons & Dragons, Dutch, Dwarf

Danish
www.DanishSingles.com
www.HappyDays.dk

Dancing
www.Dancers.Tangowire.com
www.1greatdancesite.com/ads2.htm
www.Want2dance.BigStep.com

Danske
www.Danske.Tangowire.com

Dating with No Kids attached
www.DinkLink.com
www.NoKidsPassions.com

Deaf
www.Deafs.com
www.Deafdates.com
www.DeafDate.CB.Deafs.com
www.DeafDate.net
www.DeafPassions.com
www.Deaf.meetup.com
www.DeafSinglesConnection.com
www.DeafSinglesMeet.com
www.DeafMatchInternational.com

Delaware
www.DatinginDelaware.com
www.Delaware.Tangowire.com
www.ExecutiveDelawareDating.com
www.ItsJustLunchWilmington.com
www.MeetinginDelaware.com

Deutsche
www.Deutsche.Tangowire.com

Democrats/Political
www.Democrat.Meetup.com
www.DemocratPassions.com
www.SingleDemocrats.com

Diapers
www.BeDiapered.com
www.DiaperBuddy.com
www.DailyDiapers.com
www.DiaperMatch.com

Dinner Club
www.DinnerDate.org
www.DinnerForSix.com
www.DinnerPartyDates.com
www.TakeMeToDinner.com
www.WhosForDinner.com

Disabled
www.AllDisabled.org
www.Dating4Disabled.com
www.Dawn-Disabled-Dating.com
www.DisabledCupid.com
www.Disability-dating.com
www.DisabledDatingClub.com
www.DisabledPassions.com
www.DisabledSingles.com
www.DisabledUnited.com/friends/default.aspx
www.Disabled-world.com
www.EnabledAlready.com
www.EnableLove.com
www.HiyaDisabled.com
www.LoveByrd.com
www.MingleCafe.com
www.SoulfulEncounters.com
www.Whispers4u.com

Divorced
www.DivorcedPeopleMeet.com
www.DivorcedSingles.com

Dogs
www.Activedogs.Meetup.com
www.Dogster.com
www.Doglovers.Tangowire.com
www.DogUp.com
www.LeashesandLovers.com
www.SingleDogOwners.com

Dominican
www.DominicanCupid.com
www.DominicanSingles.com

Drag Queens
www.DateaCrossDresser.com
www.Lvtg.com

Drinking
www.DrinkingBuddies.ca

Druze
www.DruzeSingles.com

Dungeons and Dragons
www.DnD.meetup.com

Dutch
www.DutchMates.com
www.DutchSingles.com

Dwarf
www.DateaLittle.com
www.DwarfDate.com

E

Ebony, Ecuadorian, Equestrian, El Salvadorian, Elvis, Egyptian, Enchanted, English, Entrepreneur, Episcopalian, Eritrean, Estonian, Espana, Ethiopian, European, Event, Everything But the Girl, Ex-Chicagoans, Executive, Exercise, Extremists, Experimental

Ebony
www.Ebony.Tangowire.com

Ecuadorian
www.EcuadorianSingles.com

Equestrian
www.EquestrianCupid.com

Egyptian
www.Arabs4Dating.com
www.EgyptianDating.com
www.EgyptianSingles.com
www.MuslimMarriageConsultants.com

El Salvadorian
www.ElSalvadorianSingles.com

Elvis
www.Elvis.Meetup.com

Enchanted
www.EnchantedDating.com

English
www.EnglishSingles.com

Entrepreneur
www.Entrepreneur.Meetup.com

Enterprise Resource Planning
www.ERP.Meetup.com

Episcopalian
www.EpiscopalianSingles.com

Eritrean
www.EritreanSingles.com

Estonian
www.EstonianSingles.com

Espana
www.Espana.Tangowire.com

Ethiopian
www.EthiopianPersonals.com
www.EthiopianSingles.com

European
www.DreamDates.co.uk
www.Europe-Dating.com
www.EuropeanMatchmaker.com
www.EastWestMatch.com
www.lJusman-Datings.com
www.PebblesOntheBeach.com
www.SerenityDating.com
www.SlowDating.com
www.TheMeetingPoint.eu

Event
www.EventBrite.com
www.ProsinTheCity.com
www.TheSocialLounge.com

Everything but the Girl
www.EBTG.Meetup.com

Ex-Chicagoans
www.ExChicagoans.Meetup.com

Executive
www.ConsciousSingles.com
www.ExecutiveAmericanDating.com
www.Executives.Tangowire.com

www.ExecutiveEasternEuropeanDating.com
www.ExecutiveEuropeanDating.com

Exercise
www.Active.com

Extremist
www.Extremist.org

Experimental
www.AvantGardeDating.com

F

Farmers, Farsi, Fat Chicks, Fetishes, Fire Fighters, Finland, Finnish, Fishing, Fitness, Florida, Football, Foreign, Freaks, Free Cycle, French, French Language, Friends, Friendster

Farmers
www.FarmersOnly.com
www.Partners4Farmers.com

Farsi
www.FarsiSingles.com

Fat Chicks
www.DatingForFatChicks.com
www.SingleFatChick.com

Fetishes
www.AllAboutFetishes.com
www.FetishFishing.com

Filipino
www.Cebuanas.com
www.FilipinoFinder.com
www.FIlipinaLadies.com
www.FilipinoSingles.com
www.MelindasPenPals.com
www.Snookys-Video.com

Finnish
www.FinnishSingles.com
www.Finland.Tangowire.com

Fire Fighters
www.CopsFirefighters.com
www.DateaFirefighter.co.uk
www.FireFighterMatch.com
www.Hot-Firefighters.com
www.SingleFirefighter.net
www.SingleFirefighters.com

Fishing
www.FishingLovers.TangoWire.com
www.FishingSingles.com

Fitness
www.FitnessDates.com
www.Fitness-Singles.com
www.Fitness.TangoWire.com

Florida
www.DatingInFlorida.com
www.ExecutiveFloridaDating.com
www.Florida.Tangowire.com
www.FloridaLuv.com
www.MeetingInFlorida.com
www.ItsJustLunchBoca.com
www.ItsJustLunchFtLauderdale.com
www.ItsJustLunchFtMyers.com
www.ItsJustLunchJacksonville.com
www.ItsJustLunchMiami.com
www.ItsJustLunchNaples.com
www.ItsJustLunchOrlando.com
www.ItsJustLunchSarasota.com
www.ItsJustLunchTampa.com
www.ItsJustLunchPalmBeach.com
www.Florida-Online-Dating.com
www.FloridaSingles.com
www.SarasotaSingles.com
www.TampaBayDating.com
www.TampaMojo.com

Football
www.FootballLovers.TangoWire.com

Foreign-Oversees
www.Blossoms.com
www.ForeignDateFinder.com

Freaks
www.FreakDating.com
www.VeganFreak.net

Free cycle
www.FreeCycle.Meetup.com

French
www.ExecutiveFrenchDating.com
www.FrenchFinder.com
www.French-Romance.com
www.FrenchSingles.com

French Language
www.French.Meetup.com

Friends
www.FriendCircle.com
www.Friends.com
www.Friends-In-Kiev.com
www.FriendsReunited.com
www.HelloNetFriends.com
www.miniclip.com/games/club-penguin/en/
www.SooperFriends.com
www.Wetties.com

Friendster
www.Friendster.Meetup.com

G

Gamblers, Gamers, Gardeners, Gay, Gay-Chubby, Gay Cowboy, Geeks, Gemini, Generation X, German, Geo, Georgia, Ghanian, Ghetto, Golden Age, Golf, Gothic, Greek, Greek Orthodox, Guatemalan, Guinean, Gujarati, Gypsy

Gamblers
www.Gamblers.TangoWire.com

Gamers
www.GaiaOnline.com
www.Gamers.Tangowire.com
www.Kaneva.com
www.SudokuAddicts.com
www.Slingo.com
www.Squidoo.com/Online—Dating

Gardners
www.Gardeners.TangoWire.com

Gay
www.Connexion.org
www.Gay.com
www.GayBearDating.com
www.GCruise.com
www.GayDardate.com
www.GayDating247.com
www.GayDatingClubx.com
www.GayLounge.com
www.GayandLesbianMatchmaker.com

www.Gay.Tangowire.com
www.Man2ManPersonals.com
www.MeninLove.com
www.OutPersonals.com
www.PlanetOut.com
www.RequestaDate.com

Gay Chubby
www.GayChubby.com

Gay cowboy
www.GayCowBoyCentral.com

Geeks
www.Geeks.TangoWire.com

Gemini
www.Gemini.TangoWire.com

Generation x
www.GenXSingles.com

Geo
www.GeoSingles.com

Georgia
www.DatingInGeorgia.com
www.ExecutiveGeorgiaDating.com
www.GeorgiaOnlinePersonals.com
www.GeorgiaPassions.com
www.GeorgianSingles.com

www.Georgia.Tangowire.com
www.ItsJustLunchAtlanta.com
www.ItsJustLunchAtlantaSuburbs.com
www.MeetingInGeorgia.com

German
www.ExecutiveGermanDating.com
www.GermanFriendfinder.com
www.GermanSingles.com

Ghanian
www.GhanianSingles.com

Ghetto
www.MyGhetto.com/join_us.php

Ghost tracking
www.Ghosts.Meetup.com

Golden age
www.GoldenAgeSingles.com

Golf
www.DateaGolfer.com
www.GolfMates.com
www.Golfers.Tangowire.com
www.IGolf.to
www.LoveBirdie.co.uk

Gothic
www.GothicDates.com
www.GothicDates.net
www.Gothic-Singles.de
www.GothicMatch.com
www.GothicMatch.com
www.GothicSoulMate.com
www.PrettyGothic.com

Greek-Greek Orthodox
www.GreekSingles.com
www.GreekOrthodoxSingles.com
www.Kapan4e.com
www.OrthodoxSingles.com
www.SexyHellenics.com
www.WorldWideGreeks.com

Guatemalan
www.GuatemalanSingles.com

Guinean
www.GuineanSingles.com

Gujarati
www.GujaratiSingles.com

Gypsy
www.GypsySingles.com

H

Hash House Harriers, Haitian, Hawaii, Hermit, Health, Hero, Herpes, Hikers, Hillbilly, Hindi, Hindu, Hip-Hop, Hispanic, Hockey, Honduran, Hong Kong, Hood, Horse Lovers, Hungarian

Hash House Harriers
www.HashHouseHarriers.Meetup.com

Haitian
www.HatianConnection.com
www.HatianSingles.com

Hawaii
www.DatingInHawaii.com
www.ExecutiveHawaiiDating.com
www.HawaiiOnlinePersonals.com
www.HawaiiCity.com/Personals
www.HawaiiSinglesNetwork.com
www.Hawaii.Tangowire.com
www.ItsJustLunchHonolulu.com
www.Nieukhoa.com
www.MeetingInHawaii.com

Health
www.HealthyBodies.Tangowire.com

Hermit
www.HermitDate.com

Hero
www.DateaHero.com/Personals

Herpes
www.Herpes-Date.com
www.HerpesMates.com

Hikers
www.Hikers.TangoWire.com

Hillbilly
www.HillBillyDating.com

Hindi
www.HindiSingles.com

Hindu
www.HinduSingles.com

Hip-Hop
www.Hip-Hop.net
www.HipHopMatchmaker.com
www.Imeem.com/tag/hiphop
www.ThatFhatass.com

Hispanic
www.AmigoPlanet.com
www.HispanicLovers.com
www.LatinFriends.com

Hockey lovers
www.HockeyLovers.TangoWire.com

Hood
www.HoodHookups.com

Honduran
www.HonduranSingles.com

Hong Kong
www.HongKongSingles.com

Horse Lovers
www.HorseLoversConnection.com
www.HorseLovers.Tangowire.com
www.ReinsandRomance.com

Hungarian
www.HungarianSingles.com

I

Icelandic, Idaho, Illinois, India, Indian, Indiana, Indonesian, Intellectual, Interracial, International Marriage, Investors Business Daily, Iran, Iraqi, Irish, Islamic, Israeli, Italian, Ivy League

Icelandic
www.IcelandicSIngles.com

Idaho
www.DatingInIdaho.com
www.ExecutiveIdahoDating.com

www.IdahoDating247.com
www.IdahoOnlineMall.com
www.Idaho.Tangowire.com
www.ItsJustLunchBoise.com
http://idaho.uscity.net/Dating/
www.LookatBoise.com
www.MeetingInIdaho.com
www.SingleIdaho.com

Illinois
www.DatingInIllinois.com
www.ExecutiveIllinoisDating.com
www.Illinois.Tangowire.com
www.MeetingInIllinois.com
www.ItsJustLunchChicago.com
www.ItsJustLunchChicagoSuburbs.com

India
www.AmbitiousIndians.com
www.DatingFunda.com

Indian
www.IndianFriendFinder.com
www.IndianSingles.com
www.PyarOnline.com

Indiana
www.DatingInIndiana.com
www.ExecutiveIndianaDating.com
www.Indiana.Tangowire.com
www.MeetingInIndiana.com

Indonesia
www.IndonesianCupid.com
www.IndonesianSingles.com

Intellectual
www.IntellectualSingles.com

Interracial
www.AfroRomance.com
www.InterracialVillage.com
www.Interracial.Tangowire.com
www.MixDate.com
www.Neep.info
www.UsHomeNow.com

International Marriage
www.ABC-Dating.net

Investors Business Daily
www.IBD.Meetup.com

Iran
www.IranSingles.com

Iraqi
www.IraqiSingles.com

Irish
www.AnotherFriend.com
http://dating.irishexaminer.com/
www.Dating-Ireland.com

www.Heart-of-Mine.com
www.IrishSinglesNetwork.com
www.Ireland.Tangowire.com
www.TheIrishWorld.com

Islamic
www.Islam.tc

Israeli
www.IsraeliSingles.com

Italian
www.ItalianFriendFinder.com
www.Italian.Meetup.com
www.ItalianSingles.com
www.ItalianSinglesOnline.com
www.ItalianSinglesConnection.com

Ivy League
www.IvySinglesDC.com
www.IvySinglesPlusDC.org

J

Jain, Jamaican, Japanese, Jehovah, Jewish, Jordanian, Journalist, Juggle

Jain
www.JainSingles.com

Jamaican
www.JamaicanSingles.com

Japanese
www.ExecutiveJapaneseDating.com
www.JapaneseDating.net
www.JapaneseHearts.com
www.JapanCupid.com
www.Japan.Meetup.com
www.Japan.Tangowire.com
www.KissTokyo.com

Jehovah
www.JW-Connect.com

Jewish
www.Frumster.com
www.Jdate.com
www.Jewishdating247.com
www.JewishFriendfinder.com
www.JewishOrthodoxSingles.info
www.JMatchConnection.com
www.StarSingles.com

Jordanian
www.JordanianSingles.com

Journalist
www.MediaBistro.com

Juggle
www.Juggle.Meetup.com

K

Kansas, Kazak, Kentucky, Kenyan, Kirghiz, Knitting, Korean, Kosovar, Kotton Mouth Kings, Kurdish, Kuwaiti

Kansas
www.DatingInKansas.com
www.ExecutiveKansasDating.com
www.Kansas.Tangowire.com
www.MeetingInKansas.com

Kazak
www.KazakSingles.com

Kentucky
www.DatinginKentucky.com
www.ExecutiveKentuckyDating.com
www.MeetingInKentucky.com
www.ItsJustLunchLousiville.com
www.Kentucy.Tangowire.com

Knitting
www.Knitting.Meetup.com

Kenyan
www.KenyanSingles.com

Kirghiz
www.KirghizSingles.com

Korean
www.ExecutiveKoreanDating.com
www.KoreanCupid.com
www.KoreanRomance.com
www.KoreanSingles.com
www.KoreanFriendfinder.com

Kosovar
www.KosovarSingles.com

Kotton mouth kings
www.KottonMouthKings.Meetup.com

Kurdish
www.KurdishSingles.com

Kuwaiti
www.CafeTropic.com

L

Laotian, Large, Latino, Latter Day Saints, Latvian, League of American Investors, Leo, Lesbians, Libra, Libyan, Lithuanian, Little People, London, Louisiana, Lutheran

Laotian
www.LaotianSingles.com

Large
www.Largeandlovely.com
www.LargeFriends.com

Latino
www.Amor.com
www.Amigos.com
www.LatinFriends.com
www.LatinoDate.com
www.Latino.Tangowire.com
www.Migente.com
www.Tangowire.com

Latter Day Saints-Mormons
www.HotSaints.com
www.LDS30Hearts.com
www.LDSHearts.com
www.LDSMingle.com
www.LDSPals.com
www.LDSPlanet.com
www.LDSRomance.com
www.LDSSingles.com
www.LDSZone.com
www.LDSSingleSaints.com
www.LDSZone.com

Latvian
www.LatvianSingles.com

League OF AMERICAN investors
www.InvestorsLeague.meetup.com

Leo
www.Leo.TangoWire.com

Lesbians
www.GirlDates.com
www.LesFemmescafe.com
www.Lesbianation.com
www.LesbianWorlds.com
www.Lesbiru.com
www.LesbianPersonalsOnline.com

Libra
www.Libra.TangoWire.com

Libyan
www.LibyanSingles.com

Little People
www.LittlePeopleMeet.com

London
www.GumTree.com

Lithuanian
www.LithuanianSingles.com

Louisiana
www.DatingInLouisiana.com
www.ExecutiveLouisianaDating.com
www.MeetingInLouisiana.com
www.ItsJustLunchNewOrleans.com
www.Louisiana.Tangowire.com

Lutheran
www.LutheranSingles.com

M

Macedonian, Maharashtrian, Mail Order, Maine, Malagasy, Malaysian, Maltese, Marathi, Marine Corp, Marriage, Married, Marthi Language, Martial Arts Movies, Maryland, Massachusetts, Mature, Mechanics, Medical Condition, Men, Mennonites, Methodist, Mexico, Michigan, Midgets, MILF, Millionaire, Military, Millionaire-Ugly, Minnesota, Mississippi, Missouri, Moldavian, Mongolian, Montana, Montengeran, Models, Moms, Mormon, Moroccan, Mountain Climbers, Movie Buffs, Mozambican, Mulatto, Music, Muslim

Macedonian
www.MacedonianSingles.com

Maharashtrian
www.MaharashtrianSingles.com

Mail-order
www.Anastasia-International.com
www.Bridesbymail.com
www.ChanceforLove.com
www.Dating-Review.co.uk
www.Romancium.com
www.Russian-Brides-Dating.blogspot.com
www.SingleWebs.com

Maine
www.DateMaine.com
www.DatingInMaine.com
www.ExecutiveMaineDating.com
www.MaineGaySingles.com
www.MaineMingles.com
www.MainePersonals.com
www.Maine.Tangowire.com
www.MeetingInMaine.com
www.SinglesofMaine.com

Marine Corp
www.MarineCorpsSingles.com

Malagasy
www.MalagasySingles.com

Malaysian
www.MalaysianSingles.com

Maltese
www.MalteseSingles.com

Marathi
www.MarathiSingles.com

Marriage
www.Dating-for-Marriage.com
www.GirlforMarriage.com
www.SeekingMarriage.com
www.Top-Marriage.net

Married
www.DatingaWife.com
www.DiscreetAdventures.com
www.LonelyCheatingWives.com
www.Married.net
www.MeetaWife.net

Marthi language
www.MarthiLanguage.Meetup.com

Martial arts movies
www.MartialArtsMovies.Meetup.com

Maryland
www.DatingInMaryland.com
www.ExecutiveMarylandDating. com
www.ItsJustLunchBaltimore.com
www.Maryland.Tangowire.com
www.MeetingInMaryLand.com

Massachusetts
www.DatingInMassachusetts.com
www.ExecutiveMassachusettsDating.com
www.GayInMa.com
www.MassachusettsOnlinePersonals.com
www.Massachusetts.Tangowire.com
www.MeetingInMassachusetts.com
www.ItsJustLunchBoston.com
www.PostClub.com

Mature
www.MatureSet.com
www.RealMatureSingles.com

Mechanics
www.LoveMechanics.com

Medical Condition
www.Prescription4Love.com

Men
www.Men.Tangowire.com

Mennonite
www.MennoniteSingles.com

Methodist
www.MethodistSingles.com

Mexico
www.MexicanSingles.com
www.Mexico.Tangowire.com

Michigan
www.DatingInMichigan.com
www.ExecutiveMichiganDating. com
www.ItsJustLunchAnnArbor.com
www.ItsJustLunchDetroit.com
www.ItsJustLunchGrandRapids.com
www.ItsJustLunchMarquette.com

www.MeetingInMichigan.com
www.Michigan.Tangowire.com

Midgets
www.LonelyMidget.com
www.MidgetSexfinder.com

Milf
www.MILF.com

Millionaire
www.MillionaireMatch.com
www.SeekingMillionaire.com
www.SugarDaddie.com

Military
www.ExecutiveMilitarydating.com
www.GiSingles.com
www.MilitaryFriends.com
www.MilitaryLovelinks.com
www.MilitarySinglesConnection. com
www.MilitarySingles.com
www.Militray.Tangowire.com
www.MilitarySweethearts.com
www.UniformDating.com
www.UsMilitarysingles.com

Millionaire-Ugly
www.Marry-An-UglyMillionaire-Online-Dating-Agency.com/

Minnesota
www.DatinginMinnesota.com
www.ExecutiveMinnesotadating.com
www.ItsjustLunchMinneapolis.com
www.ItsjustLunchStPaul.com
www.MeetinginMinnesota.com
www.Minnesota.Tangowire.com

Mississippi
www.DatinginMississippi.com
www.ExecutiveMississippiDating.com
www.MeetinginMississippi.com
www.Mississippi.Tangowire.com

Missouri
www.DatinginMissouri.com
www.ExecutiveMissouriDating.com
www.ItsjustLunchKansaCity.com
www.ItsjustLunchStLouis.com
www.MeetinginMissouri.com
www.Missouri.Tangowire.com

Montana
www.DatinginMontana.com
www.ExecutiveMontanaDating.com
www.MeetinginMontana.com

Models
www.ElenasModels.com
www.Gia.com.ua
www.ModelDatingUK.com

Moldavian
www.MoldavianSingles.com

Moms
www.Moms.Meetup.com

Mongolian
www.MongolianSingles.com

Montenegrin
www.MontenegranSingles.com

Mormon
www.MormonSingles.com

Moroccan
www.MorrocanSingles.com

Mountain Climbers
wwww.ClimbersNetwork.com

Movies
www.MovieBuffs.Tangowire.com

Mozambican
www.MozambicanSingles.com

Mulatto
www.MulattoMatch.com
www.InterracialMatchOnline.com
www.InterracialPeopleMeet.com

Music
www.MusicalSingle.com
www.Musicians.Tangowire.com

Muslim
www.Muslimo.com
www.MuslinSingles.com
www.Qiran.com

N

NASCAR, Natives, Native American, Navy, Nebraska, Nepalese, Netherlands, New Hampshire, New in Town, New Jersey, New Mexico, New York, Nevada, New Zealand, Nicaraguan, Nigerian, Niger, North America, No-Sex, Non-Smokers, North Carolina, North Dakota, Norwegian, Nudist

NASCAR
www.DatingNascarLovers.com
www.NascarMatch.com
www.Race-Date.com

Natives
www.FirstNationsDating.com

Native American
www.Bensn.com
www.NativeAmericanPassions.com
www.NativeAmericanSingles.com
www.SnagSkin.com
www.TribalSingles.org

Navy
www.NavySingles.com

Nebraska
www.ExecutiveNebraskadating.com
www.ItsjustLunchOmaha.com
www.MeetinginNebraska.com
www.Nebraska.Tangowire.com

Nepalese
www.NepaleseSingles.com

Netherlands
www.Netherlands.Tangowire.com

New Hampshire
www.DatinginNewHampshire.com
www.Directorynh.com/NHPersonalServices/NHDating.htm
www.ExecutiveNewHampshireDating.com
www.NewhampshireOnlinePersonals.com
www.MeetinginNewHampshire.com
www.NewHampshire.Tangowire.com
www.SeacoastChristiansingles.com
www.TogetherNH.com

New in town
www.NewInTown.Meetup.com

New Jersey
www.DatinginNewJersey.com
www.ExecutiveNewJerseydating.com

www.ItsjustLunchFtLee.com
www.ItsjustLunchMarlton.com
www.MeetinginNewJersey.com
www.NewJersey.Tangowire.com

New Mexico
www.DatinginNewMexico.com
www.ExecutiveNewMexicoDating.com
www.ItsjustLunchAlbuquerque.com
www.MeetinginNewMexico.com
www.NewMexico.Tangowire.com

New York
www.DatinginNewYork.com
www.ExecutiveNewYorkDating.com
www.NewYorkFriendfinder.com
www.ItsjustLunchAlbany.com
www.ItsjustLunchBuffalo.com
www.ItsjustLunchLongIsland.com
www.ItsjustLunchNewYorkCity.com
www.ItsjustLunchRochester.com
www.WeekendDating.com
www.MeetinginNewYork.com

Nevada
www.DatinginNevada.com
www.ExecutiveNevadaDating.com
www.MeetinginNevada.com

New Zealand
www.NewZealanderSingles.com
www.NewZealand.Tangowire.com
www.NZDating.com
www.SimplySolo.com

Nicaraguan
www.NicaraguanSingles.com

Nigerian
www.NigerianSingles.com

Niger
www.NigerSingles.com

No-sex
www.NoSexDating.co.uk

Non-Smokers
www.SingleNonSmokers.com
www.Non-Smokers.Tangowire.com

North America
www.NorthAmiercaSingles.com

North Carolina
www.DatinginNorthCarolina.com
www.ExecutiveNorthCarolinadating. com
www.ItsjustLunchCharlotte.com
www.ItsjustLunchRaleigh-Durham.com

www.MeetinginNorthCarolina.com
www.NorthCarolina.Tangowire.com

North Dakota
www.DatinginNorthDakota.com
www.ExecutiveNorthDakotaDating. com
www.MeetinginNorthDakota.com
www.NorthDakota.Tangowire.com

Norwegian
www.NorwegianSingles.com

Nudist
www.ClothesFree.com
www.EuroNaturist.com
www.NudistFriendfinder.com
www.NudistMatchMaker.com

O

Ohio, Oklahoma, One Night Stand, Oregon, Oriental, Orgies,
Orthodox Christian, Over-30

Ohio
www.DatinginOhio.com
www.ExecutiveOhioDating.com
www.ItsjustLunchCincinatti.com
www.ItsjustLunchCleveland.com
www.ItsjustLunchColumbus.com
www.MeetinginOhio.com
www.Ohio.Tangowire.com

Oklahoma
www.DatinginOklahoma.com
www.ExecutiveOklahomaDating.com
www.MeetinginOklahoma.com
www.Oklahoma.Tangowire.com

One Night Stand
www.EasyOneNightStand.com
www.OneNightStandDating.com

Oregon
www.DatinginOregon.com
www.ExecutiveOregonDating.com
www.ItsjustLunchPortland.com
www.MeetinginOregon.com
www.Oregon.Tangowire.com

Orgies
www.SexathonParties.com

Oriental
www.OrientalSingle.com

Orthodox Christian
www.OrthodoxChristiandating.com
www.OrthodoxSingles.com

Over 30
www.OverThirtySingles.com

P

Pagan, Pal, Pakistan, Party, Panamanian, Paraguayan, Pennsylvania, Petite, Pets, Peruvian, Pisces, Poker, Police, Polish, Polska, Polynesian, Portuguese, Presbyterian, Prison, Protestant, Professional, Public Heroes, Puerto Rican, Pug, Punk

Pagan
www.PaganFriendSearch.com
www.Pagan.Meetup.com
www.PaganPartners.com

Pakistan
www.PakistaniSingles.com
www.PyarOnline.com
www.Shadi.com

Pal
www.PalFactor.com

Panamanian
www.PanamanianSingles.com

Paraguayan
www.ParaguayanSingles.com

Party
www.CrushParty.com
www.GoldStarEvents.com
www.Going.com
www.PartyKarma.com

www.PartyParty.com
www.PlumParty.com

Pennsylvania
www.DatinginPennsylvania.com
www.ExecutivePennsylvaniaDating. com
www.ItsjustLunchCentralPennsylvania.com
www.ItsjustLunchHarrisburg.com
www.ItsjustLunchPhiladelphia.com
www.ItsjustLunchPhiladelphiaSuburbs.com
www.ItsjustLunchPittsburgh.com
www.MeetinginPennsylvania.com
www.Pennsylvania.Tangowire.com

Peruvian
www.Peruvianingles.com

Petite
www.Petite.Tangowire.com

Pets
www.DateMyPet.com
www.DatePetLovers.com
www.LovemeLovemyPets.com
www.PetDate.co.uk
www.MustLovePets.com
www.PetDatingOnline.com
www.PetPeopleFishing.com

Pisces
www.Pisces.Tangowire.com

Poker
www.PokerDating.net
www.Poker.Meetup.com
www.Pisces.Tangowire.com

Poker
www.PokerDating.net
www.Poker.Meetup.com
www.Poker-Online-Dating.com

Police
www.PoliceSingles.com

Polish
www.PolishClub.com
www.PolishDatingClub.com
www.PolishLove.com
www.PolishMarriage.org
www.PolishSingles.com

Polska
www.Polska.Tangowire.com

Portuguese
www.Amigos.com
www.CafeTropic.com
www.Portugal.com
www.PortugueseSingle.com

Presbyterian
www.PresbyterianSingles.com

Prison
www.CellBlockMail.com
www.CellBlockPals.com
www.Inmate.com
www.LadiesofThePen.com
www.Meet-an-inmate.com
www.PatrickCrusade.org/pen_pals.htm
www.PrisonPals.com

Professional
www.Professionalingles.com
www.ProfessionalSinglesClub.com
www.UpLandProfessionalSingles.com

Protestant
www.ProtestantSingles.com

Public heroes
www.Public Heros.Tangowire.com

Puerto Rican
www.PuerotRicanSingles.com

Pug
www.Pug.Meetup.com

Punk
www.HellMates.com
www.PunkBabes.net
www.PunkPassions.com

Q

Quaker, Quick

Quaker
www.QuakerSingles.org
www.FriendlySpirit.com
www.PennSingles.com

Quick
www.QuickDates.org
www.QuickDateInfo.com
www.QuickMatch.ca
www.Quick-Spark.com
www.TemeculaQuickdate.com

R

Racing, Redheads, Rednecks, Referral Only, Religion, Reptile, Rhode Island, Rich, Robust, Rocker, Romanian, Runners, Russian, Rwanda

Racing
www.RacingLovers.Tangowire.com

Redheads
www.RealmOfRedheads.com
www.RedHeadPassions.com

Rednecks
www.RedNeckandSingle.com
www.RedNeckConnect.com

Referral Only
www.OrKut.com

Religious
www.Isopersonals.com/join.htm

Reptile
www.RedTailBoa.net

Rhode Island
www.DatinginRhodeIsland.com
www.ExecutiveRhodeIslandDating.com
www.MeetinginRhodeIsland.com
www.RIsingles.com
www.RIcsf.org
www.RhodeislandOnlinePersonals. com
www.RhodeIsland.Tangowire.com
www.SImo-ri.org/simoportal
www.SingleRI.com

Rich
www.RichGuysTrophyWife.com
www.SugarDaddie.com

Robust
www.RobustSingles.com

Rocker
www.DateARocker.com

Romanian
www.RomanianSingles.com

Russian
www.AllRussianLadies.com
www.An-kor.com
www.AntonsIntro.net
www.APrettyWoman.com
www.Army-of-Brides.com
www.AuroraDate.com
www.BadRussianGirls.com
www.BlondeVenus.net
www.Blonde-Russian-Women.net
www.BlueSapphires.net
www.ChanceForLove.com
www.EasternDream.com
www.Edem-Club.Kiev.ua
www.EliteRussianWomen.com
www.Email2Female.com
www.ExoticLady.net
www.GetMarriedNow.com
www.GloriousLadies.com
www.Marriage.Amenint.com
www.Russian-Brides-Russian-Brides.com
www.RussianSingle.com
www.Russian-Women-Links.net
www.Russian-Women-Topsites.com

Runners
www.Runners.Tangowire.com

Rwandan
www.RwandanSingle.com

S

Sagittarius, Saudi, Scandinavian, School, Scorpio, Scotland, Scrap-booking, Senegalese, Senior, Separated, Serbian, She Males, Shiite, Short, Singles Events, Single Parents, Short, Sikh, Singapore, Sinhalese, Sino, Skaters, Skiers, Slavic, Slim, Slovakian, Slovenian, Smokers, Snakes, Snow Lovers, Sobriety, Social Networking, Soccer, Somolia-Kisimayo, South Asian, South Carolina, South Dakota, South Africa, South America, Spanish Language, Spanking, Speed Dating, Spiritual, Sports, Sports-Fans, STD, Srilankan, Sudanese, Surfers, Swedish, Swingers, Switzerland, Syrian

Sagittarius
www.Sagittarius.Tangowire.com

Saudi
www.SaudiSingles.com

Scandinavian
www.ScandinavianSingles.com

School
www.ClassMates.com
www.GradFinder.com

Scorpio
www.Scorpio.Tangowire.com

Scotland
www.Edinburgh.Gumtree.com
www.ScottishSingles.com

Scrap-booking
www.Scrapbooking.Meetup.com

Senegalese
www.SenegaleseSingles.com

Senior
www.AllSeniorDating.com
www.DatingForSeniors.com
www.SeniorCircle.com
www.SeniorDateConnection.com
www.SeniorDatingExchange.com
www.SeniorDateFinder.com
www.SeniorFriendFinder.com
www.Seniors.Tangowire.com
www.MeetSeniors.com
www.SassySenior.com
www.SilverFishing.com
www.SeniorPeopleMeet.com
www.SilverFishing.com
www.YourSeniorDating.com

Separated
www.SeparatedSingles.com

Serbian
www.SerbianSingles.com

She-Males
www.FindaSheMaleLover.com
www.LVTG.com
www.SheMaleDates.com
www.SheMale-Dating.net
www.SheMaleSexDates.com
www.SheMaleDatingSites.com
www.TransPassions.com
www.TsgGirlfriend.com

Shiite
www.ShititeSingles.com

Short
www.ShortSingles.com
www.Short.Tangowire.com

Sikh
www.SikhSingles.com

Singapore
www.SingaporeanSingles.com
www.Singapore.Tangowire.com

Singles Events
www.Ticket4one.com
www.SinglesEvents.com

Single Female
www.SingleFemale.net

Single Parents
www.SingleParent.com
www.SingleParentLove.com
www.SingleParentMeet.com
www.SingleParents.Tangowire.com

Singhalese
www.SinghaleseSingles.com

Sino
www.SinoSingles.com

Skaters
www.SingleSkaters.com
www.SkateLog.com

Skiers
www.FirstTracksOnline.com

Slavic
www.SlavicSingles.com

Slim
www.SlimSingles.com

Slovakian
www.SlovakianSingles.com

Slovenian
www.SlovenianSingles.com

Smokers
www.DatingForSmokers.com
www.SmokersClubInc.com
www.SmokersDateLink.com
www.Smokers.Tangowire.com
www.420Dating.com

Snakes
www.Snakes.MeetUp.com

Snow Lovers
www.SnowLovers.Tangowire.com

Sobriety
www.KeepItSimpleDating.com
www.SoberDates.com

Soccer
www.Soccer.Tangowire.com

Social Networking
www.Collegster.com

Somolia-Kisimayo
www.jhoos.com/somalia/kisimayo
www.somlove.com

South African
www.SouthAfricanSingles.com

South America
www.SouthAmericaSingles.com

South Asian
www.SuitableMatch.com

South Carolina
www.DatinginSouthCarolina.com
www.ExecutiveSouthCarolinaDating.com
www.SouthCarolinaFriendfinder.com
www.ItsjustLunchCharleston.com
www.ItsjustLunchColumbia.com
www.ItsjustLunchGreenville.com
www.MeetinginSouthCarolina.com
www.SouthCarolina.Tangowire.com

South Dakota
www.DatinginSouthDakota.com
www.ExecutiveSouthDakotaDating. com
www.ItsjustLunchGreenville.com
www.MeetinginSouthDakota.com
www.SouthDakota.Tangowire.com

Spanish
www.Spanish.Meetup.com

Spanking
www.Spanking-Ads.com

Speed Dating
www.BriefEncounters.com
www.DateSwitch.com
www.DeeperDating.com
www.EasyDates.org
www.8MinuteDating.com
www.ExcelDating.com
www.FastDater,com
www.FastLife.com
www.HurryDate.com
www.ItsJustCoffee.com
www.ItsJustLunch.com
www.RapidDatingUsa.com
www.TableforSix.com
www.TheSingleEvent.com/speeddating.htm
www.SingleintheCity.ca
www.WhentheMusicStops.com

Spiritual
www.DharmaMatch.com
www.NewAgeConnections.com
www.SpiritualRomance.com
www.SpiritualSingles.com
www.TheOsera.com
www.UniqueDatingService.com

Sports
www.GoalDating.com
www.SportsLovers.Tangowire.com

Sports Fans
www.SportsFanMatch.com
www.SportsLovers.Tangowire.com

Srilankan
www.SrilankanLovers.com

STD
www.FreeDating-Sites.com/std.html
www.StiDatingClub.com

Sudanese
www.SudaneseSingles.com

Sunni
www.SunniSingles.com

Surfers
www.SurferPersonals.com

Swedish
www.SwedishSingles.com

Swingers
www.Swinger-Heaven.co.uk
www.SwingTowns.com

Switzerland
www.SwissSingles.com

Syrian
www.SyrianSingles.com

T

Taiwanese, Tajik, Tall, Tamil, Tanzanian, Taoist, Tattoo, Teddy Bears, Telugu, Tennessee, Tennis, Texas, 3D, Thai, 30+, Thespian, Tibetan, Town Hall, Trans-Gender, Travel, Travel-Women Only, Tri-Athlete, Truckers, Tunisian, Turkish, Turkmen, Twins

Taiwanese
www.TaiwaneseSingles.com

Tajik
www.TajikSingles.com

Tall
www.HeightSite.com
www.TallConnections.com
www.TallFriends.com
www.TallPassions.com
www.TallPeople.org
www.TallPeopleNetwork.com
www.TallPeople.Tribe.net
www.TallPersonals.com
www.Tall-Singles.com
www.TallWomenDating.net

Tamil
www.TamilSingles.com

Tanzanian
www.TanzanianSingles.com

Taoist
www.TaoistSingles.com

Tattoo
www.FindaTattoo.com/links.htm
www.rankmytattoos.com/view-tattoos.html
www.TattooPassions.com
www.TattooMates.com

Teddy Bears
ww.TeddyBears.meetup.com

Telugu
www.TeluguSingles.com

Tennessee
www.DatinginTennessee.com
www.ExecutiveTennesseeDating.com
www.MeetinginTennessee.com
www.ItsjustLunchTennessee.com

Tennis
www.1stServe.com

Texas
www.DatinginTexas.com
www.ExecutiveTexasDating.com
www.MeetinginTexas.com
www.ItsjustLunchAmarillo.com
www.ItsjustLunchAustin.com
www.ItsjustLunchDallas.com

www.ItsjustLunchFtWorth.com
www.ItsjustLunchHouston.com
www.ItsjustLunchLubbock.com
www.ItsjustLunchMidland.com
www.ItsjustLunchSanAntonio.com

Text Messaging
www.clubm8.tv

Thai
www.ThaiSingles.com

Thespian
www.ThespianSingles.com

Tibetan
www.TibetanSingles.com

30+
www.35PlusDating.com
www.ThirtyPlusSingles.com

3D
www.3dee.com
www.UnclePasha.com/3d_dating.htm

Town Hall
www.TownHall.Meetup.com

Trans-Gender
www.FindaSheMaleLover.com
www.TransGendered-Personals.com

www.TransGendered.net
www.URnotalone.com

Travel
www.Club1Travel.com
www.FriendshipTravel.com
www.MeetMarketAdventures.com
www.SimplySinglesHolidays.com
www.SingleTravelIntl.com
www.TheLimeBar.co.uk
www.TravelIndoChina.com
www.TheWorldOutdoors.com

Travel Women
www.AdventurousWench.com

Tri-athlete
www.TriAthlete.com

Truckers
www.MADTrucker.com
www.SingleTruckerSearch.com
www.SingleTruckers.net
www.TruckerPassions.com

Tunisian
www.TunisianSingles.com

Turkish
www.TurkishSingles.com

Turkmen
www.TurkmenSingles.com

Twins
www.TwinsRealm.com
www.TwinsWorld.com

U

Ugandan, Ugly, Ugly Millionaires, Ukrainian, U.K. Uniform Dating, U.K. Armed Forces, Unitarian, United Kingdom, University, Uruguayan, Utah, Uzbek

Ugandan
www.UgandanSingles.com

Ugly
www.DropDeadUgly.com
www.UglyPeople.tv

Ugly Millionaires
www.Marry-an-Ugly-Millionaire
Online-Dating-Agency.com

Ukraine
www.ConfidentialConnections.com
www.Soul-2-Soul.com
www.UkrainianSingles.com
www.Ukreine.com

U.K. Uniform Dating
www.UniformDating.com

U.K. Armed Forces
www.ForcesPenPals.com

Unitarian
www.UnitarianSingles.com

United Kingdom
www.AcrossTheRoom.uk
www.BestDatingContacts.co.uk
www.Dating-Agencies-uk.co.uk
www.ExploreLove.co.uk
www.RedFaceDating.com
www.SearchLoveOnline.com
www.TopDating.com
www.Uk-Dating-Online.co.uk
www.UKFreeDating.com

University
www.UniversityLoveConnection.com

Uruguayan
www.UruguayanSingles.com

Utah
www.ExecutiveUtahDating.com
www.MeetinginUtah.com

Uzbek
www.UzbekSingles.com

V

Vacations, Varsity, Vegan, Vegetarian, Venezuela, Vermont, Veterans, Video Dating, Vintage Cars, Virginia, Vietnam, Virtual Reality Dating

Vacations
www.italiancookerycourse.com/singles-vacations.html

Varsity
www.VarsitySingles.com

Vegan
www.VeganSingles.com
www.VeganPeace.com/links/dating_socializing.htm

Vegetarian
www.GreenFriends.com
www.VeggieSingles.com
www.VeggieDate.com

Venezuela
www.VenezuelaSingles.com

Vermont
www.DatinginVermont.com
www.ExecutiveVermontDating.com
www.MeetinginVermont.com

Veterans
www.VeteransMatch.com
www.GiSingles.com

Video Dating
www.AmorMatch.com
www.BlackBook2.com
www.Browse.iFriends.net
www.DateCam.com
www.LemonTonic.com
www.LoveAccess.com
www.RxLove.com
www.SuccessfullyDating.com
www.Zazzoo.com

Virginia
www.DatinginVirginia.com
www.ExecutiveVirginiaDating.com
www.MeetinginVirginia.com
www.VirginiaFriendfinder.com

Vietnam
www.VietNamCupid.com
www.VietnameseSingles.com

Virtual Reality
www.Adelaider.com/?thread=8052
www.Date-4-free.com/
VirtualDating.htm
www.DatingVirtually.com
www.Eros.VirtualDatingAgency.com/help.php
www.Is-singles.com
www.MyPage.tsn.cc/V-Dating/
www.OmniDate.com
www.Virtualibiza.com

www.VDating.us
www.v-girl.com/vg3/
www.VirtualDatingZone.com
www.Virtual.PerfSpot.com
www.WatchWebCams.net

W

Warts-HIV, Washington D.C., Washington State, Wealthy, Welch, Werewolf, Western, West Virginia, Widespread Panic, White, White Trash, Wicca, Witches, Widow-Widowers, Wine, Wisconsin, Writers, Wyoming

Warts-Herpes
www.DatingWithh.com
www.Hpvforum.com/hpv-and-dating.asp
www.Mpwh.net

Washington D.C.
www.DatinginWashingtonDC.com
www.ExecutiveWashingtonDCDating.com
www.ItsjustLunchWashington.com
www.MeetinginWashingtonDC.com

Washington State
www.DatinginWashington.com
www.ExecutiveWashingtonDating.com
www.MeetinginWashington.com
www.ItsjustLunchBellevue.com
www.ItsjustLunchSeattle.com

Wealthy
www.WealthyMen.com

Welch
www.WelchSingles.com

Western
www.WesternMatch.com

West Virginia
www.DatinginWestVirginia.com
www.ExecutiveWestVirginiadating.com
www.MeetinginWestVirginia.com

White
www.AllWhiteDating.com
www.AllWhiteCommunity.com

White Trash
www.WhiteTrashWorld.com

Wicca
www.Mind-n-Magick.com
www.WiccaSingles.com

Wide spread panic
www.Panic.Meetup.com

Widows-Widowers
www.WidowedSingles.com
www.WidowsorWidowers.com

Wine
www.GrapeDates.com
www.WineLoversMatch.com
www.WineLoversMeet.com
www.WineLoversOnline.com

Wisconsin
www.DatinginWisconsin.com
www.ExecutiveWisconsinDating.com
www.ItsjustLunchMadison.com
www.ItsjustLunchMilwaukee.com
www.ItsjustLunchWausau.com
www.MeetinginWisconsin.com

Witches
www.WitchDating.com
www.Witches.Meetup.com
www.Witchvox.com/lx/lx_wicca.html

Writers
www.Writers.Meetup.com
www.Writers.TangoWire.com

Wyoming
www.DatinginWyoming.com
www.ExecutiveWyomingDating.com
www.MeetinginWyoming.com

X-Y-Z

Yemenite, Yoga, Y2k, Yugoslavia, Zambian, Zimbabwean, Zoroastrian

Yemenite
www.YemeniteSingles.com

Yoga
www.YogaConnect.com
www.YogaPassions.com

Y2K
www.Y2kSingles.com

Yugoslavia
www.YugoSlavianSingles.com

Zambian
www.ZambianSingles.com

Zimbabwean
www.ZimbabweanSingles.com

Zoroastrian
www.ZoroAstrianSingles.com

Index

978-0-595-47892-7
0-595-47892-1

www.ingramcontent.com/pod-product-compliance
Lightning Source LLC
Chambersburg PA
CBHW021146070326
40689CB00044B/1146